On the Fastrack

On the Fastrack

In a Buncha Easy Lessons

by Bill Holbrook

A Perigee Book

Perigee Books
are published by
The Putnam Publishing Group
200 Madison Avenue
New York, NY 10016

ISBN: 399-51181-4

Printed in the United States of America
1   2   3   4   5   6   7   8   9   10

DON'T FORGET, BOB, THE **BIG BOSS** WANTS TO SEE YOU AT 9:00 **SHARP!**

IT HAD COMPLETELY SLIPPED MY MIND.

3-23

GOOD MORNING, MS. TRELLIS.

GOOD MORNING, BOB, PLEASED TO MEET YOU!

I KNOW YOU'RE **NERVOUS** ABOUT BEING CALLED UP HERE. **PLEASE**, DON'T BE! **RELAX!**

FORGET MY **EXECUTIVE STATUS! FORGET** THESE **TRAPPINGS** OF **POWER! IGNORE** THE INTIMIDATING **DECOR** OF MY **OFFICE!**

IGNORE THE MEDIEVAL TORTURE DEVICES?

FORGET THEY EXIST!

3-24

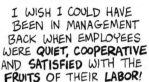

GOOD WORK, BOB! THAT WAS THE **BEST** REPORT ON COMPANY MORALE I'VE **EVER HEARD!**

BillHolbrook

"THE FIRM IS UNDERGOING A TURBULENT **ADOLESCENCE;** NEGOTIATING ITS WAY BETWEEN A SUCCESSFUL **CHILDHOOD** AND A STEADY MATURITY." **BEAUTIFUL!**

THE WRITER OF THAT REPORT WAS OBVIOUSLY SHREWD, SMART AND **OBSERVANT** OF CORPORATE **ATTITUDES** AND **AFFAIRS!** THEY SHOULD BE **CONGRATULATED!**

CONGRATULATIONS.

THANK YOU.

4-18

LAUREL, I READ AN ARTICLE TODAY THAT DISTURBED ME...

IT SAID CHILDREN REARED BY **SINGLES** ARE FORCED TO MATURE **TOO QUICKLY,** AND ARE DENIED A SHELTERED, **NURTURING ENVIRONMENT!**

BillHolbrook

DO YOU FEEL THAT'S HAPPENING TO YOU?

NO, THAT SORT OF **STIMULUS** HASN'T CONDITIONED ANY **NEGATIVE RESPONSES** INTO MY **CON-SCIOUS BEHAVIOR!**

WHEW! WHAT A **RELIEF!**

NO SWEAT.

4-19

BOB, IS WORKING FOR BUD SPORE **REALLY** AS BAD AS YOU SAY?

TRUST ME...

BUD CREATES A **CRISIS MENTALITY!** HE MAKES EVEN SLOW DAYS **STRESSFUL** BY SPREADING **ANXIETY** OVER THE ROOM UNTIL IT BECOMES **INTOLERABLE!** HE'S **NERVE-RACKING!!**

AHHHH!!

4/30

THANK GOD, HE JOGS TO RELAX!

YESTERDAY WAS THE **PITS!** THE **CAR** BROKE DOWN, I LOST MY **WALLET,** SPILLED **COFFEE** ON MS. TRELLIS, AND ENDED UP CAUSING THE **ENTIRE** COMPUTER SYSTEM AT WORK TO **SHUT DOWN!**

IT WAS JUST ONE OF THOSE DAYS WHERE YOU **WISH** YOU'D **NEVER** GOTTEN OUT OF **BED!**

5/1

GOOD THING I'M **NOT** GOING TO MAKE THE SAME MISTAKE **TODAY!**

DON'T BUY ANY OF THAT "**COMPANY LOYALTY**" STUFF THAT MS. TRELLIS IS FEEDING YOU! IN THE BUSINESS WORLD, IT'S EVERY MAN FOR **HIMSELF!**

AFTER A FEW YEARS, AN EMPLOYEE SHOULD **LEAVE** HIS COMPANY, TAKING WITH HIM EVERYTHING HE CAN — **EXPERIENCE, CONTACTS,** A GOOD NAME ON HIS **RESUME**...

5/2

...A GENEROUS SUPPLY OF POWER TOOLS...

SHHH!

Bill Holbrook

YES, LAUREL, I KNOW I'M A **PICKY** SHOPPER. IT'S JUST THAT I HAVE A HARD TIME DECIDING ON A **MAJOR** PURCHASE!

MICRO WAVE SALE

$.$$

WHEN I'M INVESTING A LOT OF **TIME,** OR **MONEY,** OR **BOTH**... I MUST BE SURE THAT WHATEVER I SELECT HAS ABSOLUTELY **NO FLAWS!**

5/3

DON'T SAY IT, LAUREL.

WHY CAN'T YOU BE THAT WAY WITH **MEN** ?

I SAID, **DON'T SAY IT!**

Bill Holbrook

OH, NO!

I HATE SPEED BUMPS.

Bill Holbrook

© 1984 King Features Syndicate, Inc. World rights reserved.

5/4

MAY I HELP YOU, SIR?

YEAH...UH, I'D LIKE— ER...UMMM...

POOKIE'S FAST FOOD

5/5

SAY, WHAT ARE YOU CALLING A HAMBURGER THESE DAYS?

THAT WOULD BE A "POOKIE SPECIAL"!

© 1984 King Features Syndicate, Inc. World rights reserved.

OUR FISH SANDWICH IS A "FINNY DELIGHT," THE CHICKEN IS THE "CLUCK-A-DOODLE-DO," AND THE APPLE PIE IS THE "YANKEE-DANDY YUMMY TREAT"!

Bill Holbrook

JEEPERS.

OH, THAT'S OUR FRENCH FRIES!

WELL, I'VE BEEN WAITING OUTSIDE ROSE TRELLIS' OFFICE FOR **FORTY-FIVE MINUTES.**

I'M NOT SURPRISED. IT'S COMMON FOR MANAGEMENT TO PLANT **SUBTLE HINTS** TELLING THE EMPLOYEE WHO'S **BOSS** AND WHO **ISN'T!**

5/7

TRELLIS IS NO EXCEPTION.

STILL, YOU HAVE TO ADMIRE HER EYE FOR **DETAIL!**

FEUDALISM MONTHLY

BOB, I WANT YOU TO ENTERTAIN A **BIG-MONEY CLIENT** TONIGHT. YOU'LL MEET HIM AT THE **OUT-OF-TOWN INN.**

ISN'T THAT WHERE ALL THE **CONVENTIONEERS** STAY?

RIGHT. HE'LL BE WEARING A LIME-GREEN **POLYESTER-BLEND** SUIT WITH SANSABELT SLACKS, WHITE LOAFERS AND A **REALLY** BAD **TOUPEE!**

...BAD TOUPEE... RIGHT...

5/8

SO HOW WILL I RECOGNIZE HIM?

HMMM... GOOD QUESTION.

AMAZING...

A **HUGE** CONTRACT... MEANING JOBS, PROFITS AND PERHAPS THE COMPANY'S **SURVIVAL**...DEPENDS ON MY ABILITY TO **KEEP** THIS CLIENT HAPPY!

5/11

SO FAR, SO GOOD.

THAT WAS A GREAT FLOOR SHOW, BOB! BUT WHEN DO WE GET SOME **REAL** ACTION?

WHEN DO WE KICK LOOSE WITH SOME WILD, UNTAMED BEAUTIES?

NOT TO WORRY!

MEETING US AT THIS RESTAURANT WILL BE TWO OF THE **FINEST** FEMALES THIS CITY HAS TO **OFFER**!

5/12

SO WOTCHA GOT IN THE **BAG**, MOM?

SEVENTEEN CANS OF MACE, DARLIN'!

BOB, YOU'VE DONE A **FINE** JOB FOR ME IN THE PAST FEW WEEKS! **NOW**, I'D LIKE **YOU** TO TAKE ON THE RESPONSIBILITY OF EDITING OUR **COMPANY NEWSLETTER!**

LOOK THIS OVER, BOB. I HAD THE ART DEPARTMENT PREPARE A **PROTOTYPE** FOR ME!

HMMM... THIS LOOKS **NICE!** GOOD GRAPHICS, SNAZZY LAYOUT, CLEAN DESIGN, **HOWEVER...**

BillHolbrook

DO YOU **REALLY** WANT TO RUN A COLOR WEATHER MAP?

5/28

I'D BE **PLEASED** TO EDIT THE COMPANY'S NEWSLETTER, MS. TRELLIS. **ONE** THING, THOUGH, YOU MIGHT **CHANGE** THE **TITLE** OF YOUR COLUMN...

BillHolbrook

WHAT'S WRONG WITH **"THE MONTHLY THOUGHT FROM ROSE TRELLIS"?**

I DON'T KNOW, BUT SOMEHOW...

5/29

IT MAKES IT SOUND LIKE AN EVENT.

ART, I'VE COME FROM MS. TRELLIS' OFFICE, AND SHE'S GIVEN ME A **PRO-JECT** THAT I NEED **YOUR** HELP ON!

IT'S A **GREAT** OPPORTUNITY FOR YOU! IT'S A **HIGH-PROFILE** JOB, AND **PERFECTLY** SUITED TO YOUR **TALENTS!**

I SUPPOSE THIS HAS SOMETHING TO DO WITH THE **GOSSIP COLUMN** YOU WANT ME TO WRITE FOR YOUR **NEWSLETTER?**

5/30

STOP DOING THIS TO ME, ART.

"On The Fastrack"

FASTRACK, INC.'S MONTHLY IN-HOUSE NEWSLETTER

INSIDE CONTENTS

NEW EMPLOYEE POLICIES
—**PAGE 2**

COMPANY FINANCIAL REPORT
—**PAGE 2**
PERSONNEL CHANGES
—**PAGE 2**

5/31

COVERAGE OF THE SOFTBALL TOURNAMENT
—**PAGES 3-12**

BillHolbrook

BillHolbrook

I GUESS YOU'RE RIGHT, LAUREL, I **AM** SCARED BY THE SUCCESSES I'VE HAD!

YOU KNOW, **JUST** LAST MARCH I WAS A SIMPLE COMPUTER OPERATOR, **MINDING** MY OWN **BUSINESS!**

BUT **NOW** I'VE BEEN THRUST INTO THE **CUT-THROAT CORPORATE WORLD,** WHERE PEOPLE DISCUSS **TAX SHELTERS** OVER LUNCH, HAVE THEIR **NAMES** ON THEIR PARKING SPACES, AND **RARELY** SEND OUT FOR **PIZZA!**

6/6

HORRORS!

A **COMPLETELY ALIEN ENVIRONMENT!**

BOB, IN ORDER TO CONQUER THESE **FEARS** OF **SUCCESS,** YOU SHOULD TRY WRITING DOWN YOUR **GOALS** IN LIFE!

6/7

1) LOVE
2) SECURITY
3) COMFORT

NO, NO, BOB...

YOU'RE BEING **TOO GENERAL.** NARROW IT DOWN! BE **SPECIFIC!**

4) AN OCCASIONAL LOBSTER DINNER.

...BETTER...

Panel 1: BOB, OUR **COMPANY PROMOTIONAL FILM** GOES INTO PRODUCTION THIS WEEK, AND I'VE HIRED A **BIG-NAME DIRECTOR** WHO'S DOWN ON HIS LUCK!

Panel 2: I'VE NEVER HEARD OF HIM, BUT HE'S APPARENTLY **WELL KNOWN**! HAVE YOU HEARD OF **LLOYD SPLICE**?

SURE! HE'S FAMOUS FOR DIRECTING **ROCK VIDEOS**!

6/18

Bill Holbrook

Panel 3: SAY WHAT?

Panel 4: THIS IS **AWFUL**! I HAD NO IDEA THIS DIRECTOR SPECIALIZED IN **ROCK VIDEOS**! HE'LL PROBABLY MAKE A **TRAVESTY** OF OUR PROMOTIONAL FILM!

Panel 5: BOB, I WANT YOU TO **PERSONALLY** WATCH THE FILMING! MAKE SURE THIS **SCRIPT** IS SHOT **EXACTLY** AS I'VE WRITTEN IT! TO THE **LETTER**!

"**FASTRACK, INC.** A COMPANY, A COMMUNITY..."

6/19

Bill Holbrook

Panel 6: "A REALLY **NEAT** PLACE TO WORK!"

...EXACTLY!

HI THERE! I'M **LLOYD SPLICE**!

I'M **BOB SHIRT**. MS. TRELLIS ASKED ME TO **OVERSEE** YOUR PRODUCTION OF OUR **PROMO FILM**!

SURE THING, BOB! IN FACT, I'M **GLAD** YOU'RE HERE. I'M HAVING **SERIOUS PROBLEMS** WITH THE SCRIPT SHE'S GIVEN ME.

6/20

SCENE 1
EXTERIOR- MORNING
HAPPY, SMILING EMPLOYEES **PARADE** INTO WORK, **CHEER-FUL** AND **EAGER** TO BEGIN ANOTHER DAY!

WHAT'S YOUR BUDGET FOR SPECIAL EFFECTS?

NOT ENOUGH, MAN.

TELL YOUR BOSS **NOT** TO **WORRY**. I'M GOING TO SHOOT THIS FILM **JUST** AS SHE'S **WRITTEN IT**!

WELL, **THAT'S** A RELIEF... BUT YOU SAID YOU HAD SOME **PROBLEMS**...

YEAH, BASICALLY, WITH THE **PROPS**. SHE'S SPECIFIED **ITEMS** THAT I'M HAVING TROUBLE **FINDING** AROUND HERE!

LIKE WHAT?

6/21

"CREATIVE, FLAWLESS WORK."

YEAH, WE MAY HAVE TO SEND OUT FOR THAT...

FLIP!
FOLD!
FLIP!

I HATE COMMUTING.

6/25

BillHolbrook

© 1984 King Features Syndicate, Inc. World rights reserved.

THIS IS A GOOD NEWSLETTER, BOB... BUT IN THE FUTURE, YOU MUST RESIST USING IT TO PROMOTE YOUR PERSONAL GOALS!

HEY! NOW WAIT A MINUTE!

SHOW ME ONE PLACE WHERE I'VE COMPROMISED MY JOURNALISTIC INTEGRITY!

THE AD ON PAGE 3.

ATTENTION! Ladies!

YOUR FACE HERE!

EXT: 5450
CONTACT BOB SHIRT!

OH... THAT.

6/26

BillHolbrook

© 1984 King Features Syndicate, Inc. World rights reserved.

THIS IS **EMBARRASSING!** HERE I AM, THE ULTIMATE RUMORMONGER, YET **NO ONE** GOSSIPS ABOUT **ME!**

7/9

WHAT CAN I DO?

JUST REMEMBER THAT PEOPLE TALK ABOUT THE UNUSUAL... THE ABNORMAL... THE UNEXPECTED...

I **KNOW!** I'VE KEPT A HIGH PROFILE! I GOT INVOLVED IN AN **OFFICE ROMANCE!** I'VE TRIED TO **BACKSTAB** MY WAY INTO BETTER POSITIONS—

YES, BUT, ART...

Bill Holbrook

EVERYONE **EXPECTS** THAT OF YOU!

FROM WHAT YOU SAY, BOB, IN ORDER TO GET PEOPLE **GOSSIPING** ABOUT ME, I SHOULD BECOME A **MODEL EMPLOYEE!**

RIGHT!

YOU CAN ACCOMPLISH THIS BY BEING **PRODUCTIVE** ENOUGH TO WIN THE **EMPLOYEE-OF-THE-MONTH AWARD!**

7/10

Bill Holbrook

YOU MEAN IT'S BASED ON **OUTPUT?** I THOUGHT IT WAS SIMPLY A **POPULARITY CONTEST!**

NO, ART... IT'S NOT!

...SO YOU JUST **MIGHT** HAVE A CHANCE!

Panel 1:
ART, HOW DO YOU INTEND TO WIN THIS PRODUCTIVITY AWARD?

I'VE GOT A PLAN, MELODY!

Panel 2:
DURING THE PAST SIX MONTHS I'VE LET **53** PROJECTS BACK UP! THAT'S A **LOT** OF WORK I'VE **PUT OFF!**

Panel 3:
THE CONTEST IS DECIDED ON THE AMOUNT OF WORK IN **ONE** DAY, SO IF I FINISH ALL THAT IN ONE **8-HOUR** PERIOD, I'M A **SHOO-IN!**

Panel 4:
WINNING THROUGH PROCRASTINATION.

7/11

Panel 5:
FASTRACK NEWSLETTER
STORY 13XP-5
ART WELDING NAMED EMPLOYEE OF THE MONTH

Panel 6:
TO THE ASTONISHMENT OF THE ENTIRE COMPANY, ART WELDING HAS WON THE MONTHLY PRODUCTIVITY AWARD.

Panel 7:
AS THE NEWS SPREAD, MANY GROPED FOR AN EXPLANATION FOR THIS COMPLETE REVERSAL OF CHARACTER.

7/12

Panel 8:
BUD SPORE, HIS SUPERVISOR, SUGGESTS UNUSUAL SUNSPOT ACTIVITY...

Bill Holbrook

MELODY, I'M WORRIED! I'M AFRAID YOUR **NIGHT CLASSES** WILL CAUSE OUR RELATIONSHIP TO...UH... CHANGE...

OH, **ART**!

DON'T BE SCARED! **REST ASSURED**, OUR EVENINGS WILL BE SPENT IN THE **SAME** WARM, **AFFECTIONATE MANNER**!

YOU'LL COME OVER, YOU'LL DRINK MY **BEER**, I'LL READ A **BOOK**, YOU'LL WATCH "**REMINGTON STEELE**"...

7/16

...I'LL FALL ASLEEP ON THE COUCH AND LAUREL WILL KICK YOU OUT!

OH, THANK **GOODNESS**!

WHY DO YOU GUYS WATCH **SPORTS** ON YOUR LUNCH BREAKS?

WELL, THEY'RE A GOOD OUTLET FOR **MODERN FRUSTRATIONS**!

WE'RE ABLE TO EXPERIENCE **WINNING** WITHOUT THE **RESPONSIBILITIES**, AND **LOSING** WITHOUT THE **CONSEQUENCES**!

7/17

I'VE GOT A **TWENTY** RIDING ON THIS.

I THINK THE LEFT FIELDER HAS A CUTE REAR END.

WADE, I WAS WONDERING IF MS. TRELLIS WOULD **COMMENT** ON THE **SUDDEN UPTURN** IN **PROFITS**. IT'S FOR THE COMPANY NEWSLETTER!

OF COURSE!

LET'S SEE, SHE ASKED ME TO ISSUE A **PREPARED STATEMENT**... YES, HERE IT IS...

7/18

SHE EXPRESSES "CAUTIOUS OPTIMISM."

THANK YOU.

BillHolbrook

SON, YOU'RE **17** NOW, AND IT'S TIME YOU THOUGHT ABOUT YOUR **FUTURE**!.. YOUR MOTHER AND I THINK YOUR HOBBY IS **NICE**, BUT—

HOBBY? MOM... DAD... YOU DON'T UNDER-STAND!

7/19

I'M A **COMPUTER EXPERT**! THAT'S MY **CAREER**! AND IT'S GOING **VERY WELL**!

BillHolbrook

I MAKE $28,000 A YEAR! I SUPERVISE TRAINED PROFESSIONALS! I'M HIGHLY RESPECTED IN MY FIELD! I'M A SUCCESS!!

BUT WHAT ABOUT COLLEGE?

WE JUST WANT TO BE PROUD OF YOU!

LISTEN UP! THE COMPANY PICNIC IS NEXT MONTH, AND THEY WANT A ROUGH ESTIMATE OF THE ATTENDANCE!

BOB, WILL YOU BE BRINGING A DATE?

UMM...

WELL, I'M NOT REAL SURE...

JUST TO BE SAFE, I'LL PUT YOU DOWN FOR TWO...

IT'S SAD WHEN YOUR SUPERVISOR HAS MORE CONFIDENCE IN YOUR SOCIAL LIFE THAN YOU DO!

7/20

© 1984 King Features Syndicate, Inc. World rights reserved.

BOB, EVER SINCE I WON THAT PRODUCTIVITY AWARD, MY LIFE HAS BEEN IN CHAOS!

PEOPLE COME TO ME WITH JOBS BECAUSE THEY KNOW THE WORK WILL GET DONE! THEY HAVE CONFIDENCE IN ME!

I'M BEING OVERWHELMED!

© 1984 King Features Syndicate, Inc. World rights reserved.

THE CURSE OF THE COMPETENT.

7/21

BOB, I WANT TO TELL YOU WHY I **DON'T** DATE **CO-WORKERS**...

IT'S BECAUSE I'M SOMEWHAT **SHY**, AND I TEND TO KEEP TO MYSELF. I TRY NOT TO BE **CONSPICUOUS**!

THE **LAST** THING I WANT IS TO SUDDENLY BECOME THE **SUBJECT** OF **COMPANY-WIDE GOSSIP**!

SHE SAID, SHE DOESN'T WANT TO BECOME THE **SUBJECT** OF COMPANY-WIDE GOSSIP!

8/3

Bill Holbrook

DON'T WORRY, BOB. **SOMEDAY** THAT **RARE BEAUTY** WILL COME ALONG FOR YOU!

WELL, LAUREL... I'VE **NEVER** BOTHERED LOOKING FOR A **RARE**, EXOTIC, ONE-IN-A-MILLION **GODDESS**!

Bill Holbrook

8/4

ALL I'VE BEEN SEARCHING FOR IS A WOMAN WHO JUST HAS A **WARM PERSONALITY**, **SMARTS** AND A **GOOD SENSE** OF **HUMOR**!

THEY'RE APPARENTLY **SCARCE**, ALSO.

LAUREL, I MET MY OLD **COLLEGE ROOMMATE** AT THE MALL TODAY, AND SHE MADE ME SO **MAD!**

8/8

SHE KNEW ME AT A TIME WHEN I WAS SEARCHING FOR **MR. RIGHT**; A MAN WHO'D SUPPORT ME FOR **LIFE!** MY ONLY GOALS WERE TO **COOK** AND **CLEAN!**

I THOUGHT SHE'D COMMENT ON HOW I'D **MATURED**, OR HOW I'D TAKEN **CONTROL** OF MY **LIFE!**

WHAT'D SHE **SAY?**

"YOU HAVEN'T CHANGED ONE BIT."

OH, NO! MS. TRELLIS WANTS TO SEE ME **AGAIN!**

SO? YOU'VE BEEN CALLED TO HER OFFICE **LOTS OF TIMES!**

8/9

...AND **NEVER** FOR ANYTHING **BAD!**

I KNOW, BUT IT'S THE **FEAR OF THE UNKNOWN!** I'M NEVER IN **CONTROL** OF THE SITUATION! I'M ALWAYS IN **UNKNOWN TERRITORY**; NEVER ABLE TO **RELAX** AND **LET DOWN** MY GUARD!

POOR BOB. LIFE FOR HIM IS A PERPETUAL FIRST DATE.

EMPLOYEE EVALUATION
1) STATE SHORT-TERM CAREER GOALS

LEAVING HERE AT 5:00.

2) STATE LONG-RANGE CAREER GOALS

8/13

GETTING HOME BY 5:30.

Bill Holbrook

WATCH WHAT YOU SAY TO MS. TRELLIS, BOB! SHE'S BEEN VERY TOUCHY LATELY!

KNOCK!

SOME DEPARTMENT HEADS HAVE BEEN PLOTTING AGAINST HER! SHE'S BECOME PARANOID ABOUT HER SECURITY!

Bill Holbrook

C'MON, WADE! SHE ISN'T THE TYPE TO DEVELOP A SIEGE MENTALITY!

8/14

CLUNK CLUNK CLUNK

8/22

8/23

HI, MOM! THIS IS LAUREL! I'M HOME FROM SCHOOL!

THANKS FOR LETTING ME KNOW, DEAR.

8/29

THE BUS WAS LATE. WERE YOU WORRIED?

WHY DO YOU ASK?

WELL, YOU ANSWERED THE PHONE ON THE FIRST RING!

NONSENSE! I JUST HAPPENED TO BE SITTING NEXT TO IT!

© 1984 King Features Syndicate, Inc. World rights reserved.

POUND! POUND! POUND!

© 1984 King Features Syndicate, Inc. World rights reserved.

RATTLE RATTLE RATTLE

8/30

ART, WHAT'S WRONG WITH YOUR TERMINAL?

WHAP!

IT'S DOWN.

HOW TO GET ON THE FASTRACK (FOR WOMEN EXECUTIVES): DOUBLE YOUR WORKLOAD.

DOUBLE YOUR HOURS.

8/31

BillHolbrook

DOUBLE YOUR EFFORTS.

BECAUSE, REMEMBER, THERE'S A DOUBLE STANDARD.

BOB, YOU'LL BE PLEASED TO KNOW THAT I'M INSTALLING AN **INCENTIVE PROGRAM** HERE!

THE **TOP EXECUTIVES** GET A $5,000 BONUS AND A COMPANY CAR, **DEPARTMENT HEADS** GET A $2,500 BONUS, AND **MIDDLE MANAGEMENT** GETS $1,000!

9/1

GREAT! AND WHAT KIND OF INCENTIVES DO THE **HOURLY WORKERS** GET?

BillHolbrook

MELODY, ARE YOU SAYING THAT BOB HAS FALLEN IN WITH A **CULT** OF YOUNG, UPWARDLY MOBILE PROFESSIONALS?

YES! THE **YUMPIES!**

9/14

THEY BREAK DOWN THEIR VICTIMS' **INDIVIDUALITY** BY MAKING THEM **TRENDY** AND WILLING TO FOLLOW ANY FAD THAT'S DEEMED "**CHIC**"!

HOW'S THAT DONE?

BY **DISORIENTING** THEIR RECRUITS WITH THEIR **BIZARRE** AND **IRRATIONAL BELIEFS!**

IT'S **TRUE!** FOOD REALLY **DOES** TASTE BETTER COOKED OVER **MESQUITE!**

LIKE MOST CULTS, THE **YUMPIES** ENCOURAGE THEIR RECRUITS TO THROW AWAY THEIR **OLD LIFESTYLES!**

THEY EXCHANGE THEIR **ROCK ALBUMS** FOR **JAZZ** AND **CLASSICAL** MUSIC! OUTDOOR **CAFES** TAKE THE PLACE OF **FAST FOOD!** HEALTH **SPAS** REPLACE PICKUP BASKET-BALL GAMES!

AT THAT POINT, THE CONVERT DRAWS OUT ALL THEIR **SAVINGS** AND TAKES THE **FINAL STEP!**

WELCOME YUMPIES

VACANCY

BY GIVING IT TO CHARITY?

NO. BUYING A BMW.

9/15

...AND NOW, THE MASTER OF MOTIVATION, RON TOPSPIN!

HELLO, YUMPIES! HOW DO YOU FEEL?

RADICALLY TRENDY AND PROUD OF IT!

YES! AND HOW DID YOU GET THAT WAY?

9/17

BY ADOPTING YOUR SUCCESSFUL LIFESTYLE!

YES! AND HOW DO WE REMAIN CONSISTENT WITH THE YUMPIE WAY OF LIFE?

BY SHOUTING OUT ANSWERS IN UNISON!

WONDERFUL!

...WILL THE MAN IN THE HERRINGBONE BLAZER PLEASE COME DOWN...

ARE THE YUMPIES IN THERE, MELODY?

YES! THEY'RE RECRUITING NEW MEMBERS!

...WILL THE WOMAN IN THE LINEN BLOUSE PLEASE COME DOWN...

WHEN DO WE RESCUE BOB FROM THEM?

FIRST, WE HAVE TO MAKE SURE HE'S IN THERE!

...WILL THE MAN IN THE PERMANENT PRESS ENSEMBLE PLEASE COME DOWN!

NOW WHAT?

FRONTAL ASSAULT. ON THREE!

9/18

MELODY, I'M SO GLAD WE CAN **TOUCH BASE** LIKE THIS!

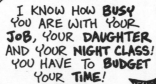

I KNOW HOW **BUSY** YOU ARE WITH YOUR **JOB**, YOUR **DAUGHTER** AND YOUR **NIGHT CLASS**! YOU HAVE TO **BUDGET** YOUR **TIME**!

SO, HERE'S A **TOAST** TO THE **THING** THAT LETS US **PARTAKE** OF EACH OTHER'S COMPANY!

TO YOUR **VCR**!

Bill Holbrook 9-24

ART, DO YOU **ALWAYS** HAVE TO BE SO CYNICAL?

CAN'T YOU **JUST ONCE** SEE THE **BRIGHT** SIDE OF **HUMAN NATURE**?

BUT I **DO**, BOB!

Bill Holbrook

9/25

WHEN I MEET SOMEONE, I TRY TO SEE THEM AS BEING **GOOD** AND **MORAL** AND GOVERNED BY **VIRTUE**!

...AND WONDER WHAT **AWFUL TRAUMA** MADE THEM THAT WAY!

SUCCESSFUL SUPERVISORS SHOW A **PERSONAL INTEREST** IN THEIR EMPLOYEES!

THEY HOLD REGULAR **GRIPE SESSIONS**, ARRANGE **SOCIAL GATHERINGS**, AND DEVELOP **ONE-TO-ONE RELATIONSHIPS!**

9/26

AS FOR **ME**, I'M CONTENT JUST TO SEE THEY'RE STILL ON THE PREMISES.

HOW TO GET ON THE FASTRACK (IF YOU'RE A LATCHKEY CHILD): LEARN FROM BOOKS.

9-27

LEARN FROM TELEVISION.

LEARN FROM ADULTS AROUND YOU.

WELL, TWO OUT OF THREE...

Panel 1: WELL, BOB'S GONE UPSTAIRS TO SEE ROSE TRELLIS AGAIN!

Panel 2: YOU'VE SEEN IT, MELODY... WHAT'S IT LIKE ON THE EXECUTIVE FLOOR? IT'S A JUNGLE UP THERE.

Panel 3: A REAL COMPETITIVE ENVIRONMENT, HUH? NO, IT'S A JUNGLE.

9/28

Panel 4: LAUREL, HERE'S AN INTERESTING GAME TO PLAY WITH A COLA BOTTLE!

9-29

Panel 5: ON THE BOTTOM IS THE NAME OF THE CITY IT CAME FROM! IT'S FUN TO SEE HOW FAR AWAY IT'S TRAVELED!

Panel 6: YEAH, BOB! MY MOM AND I PLAY A SIMILAR GAME, ONLY WE DON'T USE COLA BOTTLES.

Panel 7: WE USE THE POSTMARKS ON MY DAD'S ALIMONY CHECKS!

THE TREND IN COMPUTERS TODAY IS TO MAKE THEM MORE **ACCESSIBLE** TO THE GENERAL PUBLIC.

ALREADY, COMPUTERS HAVE CEASED TO BE THE **PRIVATE PLAY-THINGS** OF NERDS AND **HACKERS**!

Bill Holbrook

FRANKLY, I FIND THE WHOLE SITUATION APPALLING.

10-3

MEMO

FROM: BUD SPORE

10-4

TO: COMPUTER DEPARTMENT STAFF.

Bill Holbrook

RE: DISPOSAL OF FOOD EATEN AT DESKS.

HOW TO GET ON THE FASTRACK (FOR SINGLE PARENTS): BUDGET YOUR TIME.

BUDGET YOUR MONEY.

BUDGET YOUR ENERGY.

10-5

THIS IS WHERE THE PRINCIPLE OF DEFICIT SPENDING COMES IN.

ZZZZZz...

ART, I'M TIRED OF YOUR ADDICTION TO SPREADING GOSSIP!

BREAK THIS HABIT NOW!

NO, BUD. YOU'VE GOT IT WRONG...

WITH ART, GOSSIPING ISN'T A HABIT; IT ISN'T A COMPULSION...

10-6

IT'S A JOB DESCRIPTION!

THIS IS MY **FAVORITE TIME**! I'M **HOME** FROM SCHOOL, THE **CHORES** ARE DONE, AND MOM'S NOT DUE BACK FOR TWO HOURS! I'M **ON MY OWN**!

CREAK!

HMM, THAT'S **ODD**! A DISTURBING **NOISE** COMING FROM MY **MOM'S BEDROOM**!

10/8

I'LL JUST DEAL WITH THIS PROBLEM IN MY **USUAL FASHION**!...

VOLUME CONTROL!

© 1984 King Features Syndicate, Inc. World rights reserved.

LATCHKEY KIDS ANONYMOUS. MAY WE HELP YOU?

YEAH. I'VE GOT A PROBLEM...

FINE! IS IT AN **ACCIDENT** THAT HAS TO BE CLEANED UP **BEFORE** YOUR PARENT GETS HOME? IS THERE A **STRANGE MAN** AT YOUR **DOOR**? DID YOU LOSE YOUR **KEY**?

10/9

I HEARD A NOISE IN ONE OF THE BEDROOMS.

NO SWEAT! WE'LL SEND A DETAIL RIGHT OVER!

MARVELOUS ORGANIZATION! THEY'VE HELD LECTURES ON "**PARENTAL GUILT**: HOW TO USE IT TO YOUR ADVANTAGE."

© 1984 King Features Syndicate, Inc. World rights reserved.

O.K., LET'S FIND OUT **WHAT'S** MAKING THAT **NOISE** IN THERE! YOU OPEN THE **DOOR**, AND I'LL LEAD THE **CHARGE!**

RIGHT!

ONE... TWO... THREE!!

AAGH!

AAAGH!

MOM.

I CAME HOME EARLY. I HAD THE FLU.

10/12

HOW TO GET ON THE FASTRACK (IF YOU'RE A YUPPIE): BE AMBITIOUS!

BE DARING-!

10/13

BE RUTHLESS!

BUT FOR GOD'S SAKE, DON'T WORK UP A SWEAT!